D0857783

To _____

_____

From _____

_____

First published in Great Britain in 2004 by
English Heritage in association with Thames House Books.
Copyright ©2004 Thames House Books/English Heritage
Illustrations copyright ©2004 (see page 64)

Reprinted 2005

ISBN 1 85074 893 4

A CIP catalogue record for this book is available from the
British Library.

JOHN W. RUSSELL

Printed and bound in China

THE
STONEHENGE
STORY

Introduction

Stonehenge: a name that evokes awe and wonder as it fires the imagination and speaks to the soul. Stonehenge is unique, a wonder of the world with nothing like it anywhere else on the globe. The product of almost a millennium and a half of development from earthwork to stone sanctuary, it served generations of our Neolithic and Bronze Age ancestors as temple, calendar and nexus with the world of their ancestors. Unique though it is, it stands near the centre of a veritable metropolis of antiquity: other ritual sites in the region include Avebury Stone Circle, Silbury Hill and West Kennet Long Barrow. And it is a guardian of secrets. For while we have a reasonable idea of how it was built, much of its purpose remains a mystery.

In seeking to tell the story of Stonehenge, this book places it in the context of other surrounding prehistoric sites. For clarity, these will be dealt with in chronological order; thus Stonehenge itself will appear as part of the sequence set out in the timelines on page 8/9.

Stonehenge – the name

The name Stonehenge may be derived from
the Old English for stone gallows, or might
mean 'stones hanging in the sky'. 'Henge'
has gone on to acquire the meaning of a
circular monument of wood or stone that
resembles Stonehenge. More specifically, in
archaeological terms, a henge is defined as
comprising a circular ditch with a bank
outside and one or more entrances. Within
this defining enclosure, there can be circles
or groups of posts and/or stones. The basis
of Stonehenge resembles what is known as a
causewayed enclosure – a circular ditch with
gaps or 'causeways' separating individual
segments of ditch. It is a form that dates
from around 4000 BC, many examples of
which were constructed until 3000 BC.

Stonehenge in its historical context

Dating techniques put the origins of Stonehenge at about 3050 BC. To gain a better appreciation of its historical context, it is helpful to take a wider look at the surrounding area and go much further back in time. It is also informative to consider Britain's population throughout the active life of Stonehenge. Inevitably this is a matter of conjecture, but a figure of around 100,000 has been estimated for the period in which it was begun, rising to perhaps 250,000 by its final phase of use. Approximate though these figures are, it is clear that the population was very small in relation to the effort required to build Stonehenge and all the other ritual sites in the area.

Timelines for Stonehenge and surrounding sites

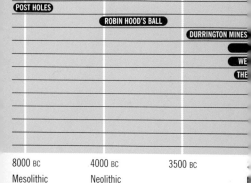

Mesolithic	Neolithic	
8000 BC	4000 BC	3500 BC

POST HOLES

ROBIN HOOD'S BALL

DURRINGTON MINES

WE

THE

8000 BC	4000 BC	3500 BC
Mesolithic	Neolithic	

The map on the following pages shows most of these sites, as well as the many barrows in the same area.

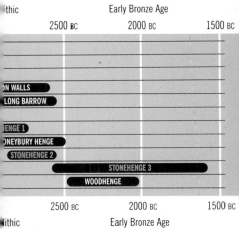

ithic	Early Bronze Age		
	2500 BC	2000 BC	1500 BC

N WALLS
LONG BARROW

ENGE 1
ONEYBURY HENGE
STONEHENGE 2
STONEHENGE 3
WOODHENGE

	2500 BC	2000 BC	1500 BC
ithic	Early Bronze Age		

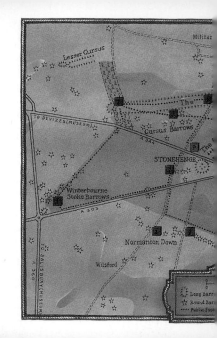

TO MARLBOROUGH

Durrington
Walls

Woodhenge

A 345

Old King
Barrows

New King
Barrows

A 303

P

Vespasian's
Camp

Amesbury

Site of
Coneybury
Henge

600 ft
660 yd
Information
Board
National Trust
area

N

A ritual landscape

The term 'ritual landscape' was coined to describe the groupings of Neolithic and Early Bronze Age monuments found across southern England, particularly the great concentrations of earthworks around (and including) Stonehenge and Avebury. It was applied to ritual or ceremonial sites as a way of distinguishing them from sites that related to everyday life, such as the homes people lived in. These were the special places reserved for periodic community meetings and, very importantly, they were concerned with rites of passage, especially death and the process of assisting the dead on the journey from the world of the living to the world of the ancestors.

The establishment of sites for such special

purposes begs the question of why a particular location was selected – what did that place have that made it suitable for life's (and death's) key moments? This is one of the mysteries that surrounds Stonehenge. The reasons may of course be practical as well as spiritual. If the original purpose concerned the provision of a meeting place, it would need to be easy to find. The high plateau of Salisbury Plain may have qualified as an adequate landmark, and it might have been on or near an established route, as it still is today. And if separation between the domain of the living and the domain of the ancestors was a requirement, then again, perhaps the higher land distanced it from the more sheltered, and therefore more inhabited, lowland.

Mesolithic remains

One piece of evidence has emerged that might help to explain Stonehenge's location. Across the A344, in the present day car park, four pits were discovered. Three were found in a row, and later a fourth came to light during building work about 100m away. It is thought they had been dug to accommodate pine posts about 600mm to 800mm in diameter. As a single row, it is difficult to suggest a practical purpose for them, so the theory has emerged that they must have had a religious or ritual function. Radiocarbon dating supported by pollen analysis dates them to between 8500 and 7650 BC – four to five millennia before Stonehenge! More conjecture, but perhaps it was already known as a 'special' place.

Robin Hood's Ball

After the Mesolithic era post-holes, this is the earliest site in the area, dating from around 4000 BC. Located about 2.3km (1.5 miles) north-north-west of Stonehenge, it is a causewayed enclosure comprising two irregular rings of bank and ditch, enclosing an area of roughly 1 hectare (2.5 acres). About 50 such enclosures have been found across southern and eastern England. Some of them have yielded human remains, mostly skulls, suggesting they played a part in funerary rituals. These sites are thought to have been used as more general-purpose meeting places as well, fulfilling the roles nowadays performed by town halls, courts and possibly churches. They were the product of a largely nomadic culture.

Durrington Mines and Walls

Flint was the main material used for tools and hunting weapons in Neolithic times. Seams of flint occur in chalk areas, and in 1952 a sewer trench at nearby Durrington cut through a flint mining area that goes back to about 3400 BC. Pits had been dug to exploit seams just below the surface and shafts sunk to reach a deeper seam.

A more dramatic discovery at Durrington was a large earthwork in the form of an oval bank about 30m (100ft) wide at its base and 3m (10ft) high. Excavations nearby revealed evidence of two circular timber structures dating from around 2450 BC. The one illustrated below, left, was 14.5m (48ft) across while the other (below, right) measured 39m (128ft) in diameter.

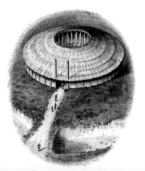

Long Barrows

Throughout the chalk landscapes of the country, the Neolithic people buried their important dead in long barrows. From a known total of over 200 throughout these areas, no fewer than fifteen are to be found within a 5km (3 miles) radius of Stonehenge, a greater density than anywhere else. They are significant structures, ranging in length from 20m (65ft) to 80m (265ft) and up to 3m (10ft) high. Their width varied from about one third to one sixth of the length, some being parallel sided while others tapered, the greatest width being at the entrance end. The best-preserved example near Stonehenge is at Winterbourne Stoke, at the junction of the A303 and A360. Long barrows date from 4000 to 3000 BC.

The Cursus

This extraordinary earthwork is perhaps the most puzzling legacy of prehistoric times in the area. It lies approximately 800m (875 yards) north of Stonehenge. As can be seen from the map on pp 10/11, it stretches a great distance, being about 2.8km (1.75 miles) long. Its width averages 90m (100 yards), the edges being marked by a small bank with a ditch outside. At its western extremity it is closed by a rounded end where the ditch and bank were deeper and higher than elsewhere. At the eastern end it is aligned on an earlier long barrow. There are a few similar earthworks; the mystery is their purpose. It is thought they were built for ritual processions, perhaps symbolising the journey of the dead into the next life.

The Ultimate Henge

Mention of ritual processions is a good way to introduce us to Stonehenge itself. About the time the sarsens were being erected (see p 36ff), the processional Avenue was marked out by means of a low bank and ditch on each side. In fact it was probably the route these stones took into the henge. But the Avenue really came into its own at the main festivals, especially Midsummer. The course of the Avenue can be traced almost down to the River Avon (see map pp 10/11), probably the location of the nearest settlement. Those taking part in the ceremony processed their way uphill in an arc-shaped route that made its final approach to the stones from the north-east, right on the alignment of the rising sun on

Midsummer's Day. Arriving at the towering stones as the sun came up must have been an awe-inspiring moment. The procession would have passed the Heel Stone (or stones – there may have been another), pictured below, just before entering the henge.

The layout of Stonehenge

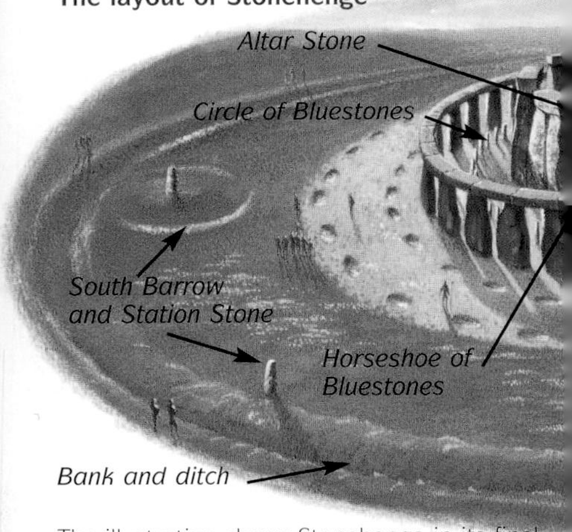

Altar Stone

Circle of Bluestones

South Barrow
and Station Stone

Horseshoe of
Bluestones

Bank and ditch

The illustration shows Stonehenge in its final
form, looking from east to west.

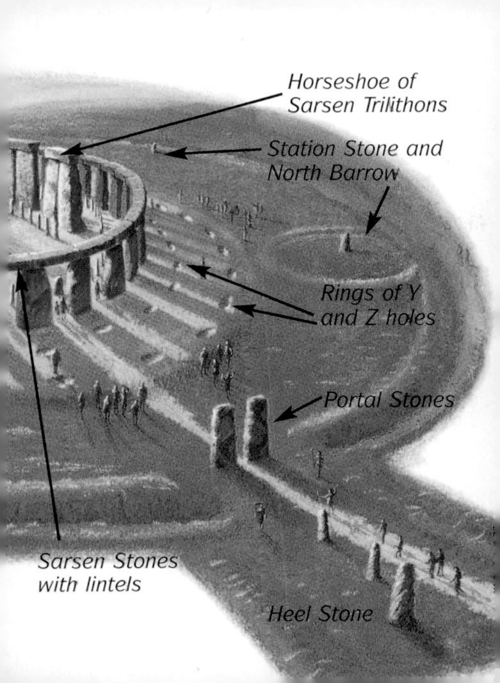

Horseshoe of
Sarsen Trilithons

Station Stone and
North Barrow

Rings of Y
and Z holes

Portal Stones

Sarsen Stones
with lintels

Heel Stone

Stonehenge today

In contrast to the illustration on the previous page, this aerial photograph

shows the stones as they are today, for comparison. Note however that this view looks the other way, from west to east.

Building Stonehenge: the first phase

As previously noted, Stonehenge was begun around 3050 BC. The initial phase comprised a circular earthwork of ditch and bank just over 100 metres (327ft) across. Within the bank a ring of 56 holes was dug, round pits in the Chalk with steep sides and flat bottoms, forming a circle 86.6m (284ft) across. To begin with they held timber posts, but some at least were later used for cremation burials. They are known as the Aubrey Holes after their discoverer John Aubrey (1626-97). Today they are marked by cement discs set into the grass.

The earthwork had two entrances, the principal of which aligns with the midsummer sunrise, to the north-east. A smaller entrance lay in the south of the circle. There is no evidence of any structure existing during this phase, but there may have been one, perhaps like that at Woodhenge (see p 57). Signs of this could have been obscured by later developments.

The first Stonehenge, showing the Aubrey Holes inside the ditch. The main entrance is at lower right.

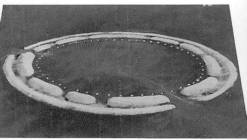

Building Stonehenge: the second phase

The first phase lasted about 150 years. The second occupied the three centuries from 2900 BC to 2600 BC, and is defined by the introduction of timber settings. Excavations have revealed a complex array of post-holes, concentrated at the centre, towards the south entrance and at the main entrance. There is insufficient clarity of pattern in the holes to allow us to know what the structures were.

By the second phase, the ditch had started to fill up naturally as the earth settled. It was also used for cremation burials, as the Aubrey Holes had been. This is one of the indicators that ritual significance was attributed to the site.

There is evidence of settlement within a

kilometre of the henge during this period, and a substantial palisade fence between the two. This indicates a formal division of the land; some who study this age believe such a layout affirms the idea of separate domains for the living and the ancestors.

The timber settings are indicated by the known post-holes.

Building Stonehenge: the third phase (1)

So far we have looked at Stonehenge in its earth/chalk period, the timber era, and in about 2600 BC the first stones arrived. These were the Bluestones, and their arrival tells us something about the people of that time. The population may have been very small, but trading over long distances had already become established, and accounts for some of the wealth of the people in the Stonehenge area. By this time, people were becoming more settled and less nomadic, so farming may also have contributed to their prosperity. Clearly they were in a position to invest a great deal in their henge.

About 80 Bluestones, averaging at least four tons each, were transported from the Preseli Mountains. Why they were chosen we do not know, but it may be related to why they are called Bluestones. When their surface is chipped away, they reveal a blue colour, speckled with white. Perhaps this feature was seen as indicative of some special significance about the stones, which justified bringing them such a distance.

Their likely route started overland, probably on rollers or sledges, to Milford Haven. From there they were taken on rafts along the South Wales coast, across the Bristol Channel and up the Avon and Frome rivers to a place near the present-day town of Frome. An overland stretch of about 10km (6 miles) then took them to the River Wylye and so by raft to Salisbury, then up the Salisbury Avon to West Amesbury, and a final mile or so uphill to the henge.

The Bluestones were firstly arranged in a double crescent at the centre of the circle. Their positioning was at roughly 90 degrees to the main entrance; thus they were not set to face the midsummer sunrise. This somewhat puzzling alignment can perhaps be accounted for by the idea that they were intended to form a complete circle or circles. However, we cannot know.

Most of the Bluestones have disappeared over the course of time, with only eighteen remaining. Of these, just two have been dressed to shape (see p 41), and are thought to have been used as lintels. This presents another curiosity, as none of their known arrangements at Stonehenge indicates that they were employed in this way. We can only conjecture about other possible uses for them: one school of thought is that some of the Bluestones were used elsewhere before they were brought to Stonehenge.

The Bluestones in their original setting.

Building Stonehenge: the third phase (2)

Two to three hundred years on from the arrival of the Bluestones, construction of the Sarsen Stone Circle began. This is the moment that could be called the great leap forward for Stonehenge: the point at which it scaled up from impressive to massive. From dealing with blocks of stone around four tonnes each, this phase involved the manipulation of slabs of 25 tonnes or more. While the sarsens were relatively local in origin, moving 30 of them the 30km (19 miles) from the Marlborough Downs represented an unprecedented feat of prehistoric transport. In addition, the 30 lintels at about seven tonnes each were no small extra.

The Heel Stone viewed through the Sarsen Circle at Midsummer sunrise.

In addition to the Sarsen Circle, a batch of even more enormous stones completed the design, in the form of a horseshoe of five 'trilithons' set within the circle. The ten uprights weigh in at about 45 tonnes each, and are capped by massive lintels. Studies in recent times have established that to move these stones up the steepest hill on the route would have needed about 500 people, plus another 100 to lay the rollers and keep the stone on course. It has also been estimated that if all 600 people had been continuously employed over the whole route, it would have taken more than a year to complete the journey. With the Sarsen Circle and the trilithons erected, Stonehenge gained its familiar look, although the position of the Bluestones at this stage is not known.

Stonehenge with the Sarsen Circle and trilithons in place. The main entrance was marked by a line of three Portal Stones, plus the Heel Stone (and possibly another like it) a little further out.

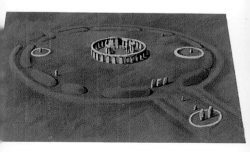

The sarsen phase of Stonehenge displays refinements that are not found anywhere else amongst the prehistoric stone monuments of Europe, outside the Mediterranean. One is that all the stones have been squared and dressed to shape, accomplished by pounding the surfaces with stone hammers. (Bronze chisels came into use during this time, but would not have been durable enough to make any impression on such hard stone). Secondly, the lintels were secured to the uprights by mortice-and-tenon joints worked from the solid stone (see top of stone, opposite) and to each other by vertical tongue-and-groove joints.

The picture opposite shows one of the two dressed and grooved Bluestones with a trilithon upright behind.

A third facet of their sophistication is the way the lintels are shaped to the curve of the circle. Getting just the right degree of curve on each individual stone so that the completed circle presented a flowing line is an extraordinary achievement. The trilithon lintels exhibit a device to deceive the eye: the sides are angled so as to make them look vertical to an observer inside the horseshoe formed by these stones. In other words, they are shaped to compensate for the natural perspective. These are refinements that are unique to Stonehenge. This final phase of construction lasted about 700 years, until approximately 1600 BC.

One of the trilithons silhouetted against the evening sky.

The layout of the other stones underwent a number of rearrangements during this period. The Bluestones were placed in at least three configurations, culminating in a circle between the sarsens and the trilithons, and a horseshoe within the trilithons. About 1700 BC two new circles of holes were dug outside the Sarsen Circle. Referred to as the Y and Z holes, their intended use is not known, but the assumption is that they may have been intended for yet another setting of the Bluestones. In the event, they were not used and are no longer visible.

Adjustments were also made to the peripheral, but no less important stones. As mentioned, when the sarsens were erected, three Portal Stones guarded the main entrance. Later in the final phase, they were reduced to two. One of these remains, no longer standing, at the entrance. Today it is referred to as the Slaughter Stone, arising out of a past belief that human sacrifices were made at Stonehenge.

The Altar Stone (see diagram pp 24/5) stood at the heart of the henge in its final phase. A dressed block of sandstone, it was positioned inside the horseshoes of Bluestones and trilithons, facing the main entrance, and therefore aligned to greet the rising sun at midsummer. Like the Bluestones, it was transported from Milford Haven. At about 5m (16ft) long, in size it was between the Bluestones and the sarsens. Today it is buried beneath a fallen trilithon. Its central position implies ritual importance, but that cannot be verified.

Erecting the stones

Getting the sarsens to Stonehenge was one thing; erecting them was quite another. The method cannot be known for sure, but might have been as follows. For the uprights, foundation pits were dug and the stone manoeuvred on rollers so that one end overhung the hole. The other end was levered up, wedged with timbers, levered up a little more, wedged again and so on until it tipped into the pit. Then, using the same process of lever and wedge, the stone was gradually moved towards the vertical. Lastly, with props to prevent it falling back, teams of men hauled on ropes from the other side until the stone was upright. The rest of the pit was filled in to secure the stone. With the sarsens shaped, the hammer-stones could be used to form part of the packing.

For the lintels, leverage remained the chief principle. Once they were positioned alongside a pair of uprights, each end was levered up in turn and secured with timber packing. A 'crib' or wooden platform would have been built around the uprights, with a further deck added each time the lintel was raised to a new level. This provided a secure surface for the labourers to work on – the prehistoric equivalent of scaffolding. When the lintel had been elevated to be in line with the top of the uprights, further leverage from ground level moved it sideways and it would be fitted on to the mortice-and-tenon to fix it in place.

An early morning view of the stones

Changing times

The question that inevitably comes to mind is why did Stonehenge cease to be a place of such importance, and allowed to fall into ruin? Categorical assertions are dangerous as we simply do not know enough to make them. But we can make some reasonable deductions that can assist our understanding.

Stonehenge was an active, almost continually developed site, for about 1,500 years. At its inception, people still pursued a lifestyle that was at least partially nomadic, although rudimentary farming, and a consequent degree of settlement, had begun. As we have seen (p 12), this society therefore required a forum for the large, periodic gatherings needed to perform functions such as weddings, funerary rites and other ceremonies, along with the need to debate matters of community interest.

1,500 years later, society had become much more settled, as a consequence of which communities became more localised and, in effect, more inward looking. So there was less need for the huge annual or quarterly gatherings of former times. Their rituals and routines seem to have scaled down proportionately. Life had moved on; the increasingly agricultural activities of a growing population led to encroachment upon the ritual landscape. In the Middle Bronze Age (around 1300 BC), the area was transformed into a network of little square fields.

Stonehenge therefore fell into decay. Some of this might have been due to natural causes: for example, we know that many of the sarsens stood in dangerously shallow holes and probably fell over quite early on. Given the absence of naturally occurring building stone in the vicinity, it became a local quarry. The Bluestones were especially vulnerable, being both smaller and more brittle than the sarsens. In more recent times, it became common practice for curious visitors to break off fragments of the stones to take away as souvenirs.

Stonehenge was in private hands until 1918, when it was given to the nation. Since then about half the site has been excavated and some of the leaning and fallen stones have been straightened or re-erected.

Coneybury Henge and Woodhenge

It is intriguing to realise that Stonehenge was not the only focus of major construction in the vicinity, for two other contemporary henges were built in the period from about 3000 BC to 2000 BC. Coneybury Henge is the earlier, and is located south-east of Stonehenge. Its presence only came to light through aerial photography.

Woodhenge, near Durrington, took the form of a circular earthwork enclosing a huge, oval wooden structure. The illustration opposite shows how it might have looked, based on the post-hole evidence at the site.

A grave containing the body of a three-year-old child was found near the centre, whose skull had been split before burial, suggesting human sacrifice.

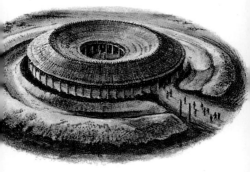

Round Barrows

The people of the Early Bronze Age favoured round barrows to bury their dead. Within a radius of 3km (2 miles) around Stonehenge, more of them can be found than in any other area of the same size in Britain. They tend to be placed in linear cemeteries that are often sited along the crest of a ridge. One of the longest is on Normanton Down, about 800m (0.5 miles) south of Stonehenge (see pp 10/11). That so many were built within sight of Stonehenge is thought to be deliberate, perhaps another reflection of its special status as the focal point of a ritual landscape. Round barrows were built in a variety of styles, descriptively named as bowl-barrows, bell-barrows, pond-barrows and disc-barrows.

The Druids

Much has been made of druidic connections with Stonehenge. This goes back to John Aubrey's suggestion three hundred years ago that the stone circles were Druid temples, and it has been believed ever since. However, it is now known that this idea is false. What we do know about the Druids comes from classical writers such as Julius Caesar, who tell us that they were a Celtic priesthood that flourished in Britain at the time of the Roman conquest and perhaps for a few centuries before. By then the stones had been standing for two thousand years and were probably already at least partly ruined. It is possible though that the Druids 'adopted' the stones long ago.

Number crunching!

5,000 years: lifetime of Stonehenge

1,500 years: length of time it was in use

164: approx. total number of stones used in final phase

1,875 tonnes: approx. total weight of stones

240 miles: the distance the Bluestones were transported to reach Stonehenge

200: the number of people needed to pull one sarsen upright

53,000 cubic feet: the volume of chalk in Winterbourne Stoke long barrow

340: number of round barrows in area around Stonehenge

c.1,000,000 man-hours: labour required to build Durrington Walls earthwork

Man-hours required to build Stonehenge: incalculable!

The spirit of Stonehenge

Today the fascination of Stonehenge is undiminished. If anything it is greater, as the multiplicity of theories it spawns captures the imagination of more and more people.

There is a dichotomy about Stonehenge: on the one hand, these secretive sentinels stand firm against our attempts to interpret them, while on the other they speak volumes about our ancestors of long ago. Though their means were limited compared with ours today, their resolve in achieving what was clearly of utmost importance to them stands in stark contrast to our impatient generation. We should not make the mistake of calling them primitive.

These were a people whose view of life was so different from ours. For them, earthly life only represented one stage in the totality of their existence. The idea that the end of this life led inevitably to the next seems to have been as natural as breathing.

For all our secular sophistication today, if one stands amid the stones and lets the imagination loose, perhaps this idea will come back into focus; for while our mind seeks to subsume such a notion, our soul, given half a chance, just might beg to differ.

Sarsen trilithon at night

Acknowledgements

Text written by Colin Nutt. Of the many books used for reference, the English Heritage Guide Book Stonehenge and Neighbouring Monuments (Edited by Ken Osborne) and Britain BC by Francis Pryor, were especially helpful.

Picture credits:
All photographs and illustrations copyright English Heritage.

Designed & produced by Viners Wood Associates

JOHN W. RUSSELL